COOL
CLIVE

MICHAELA MORGAN

Illustrated by Dee Shulman

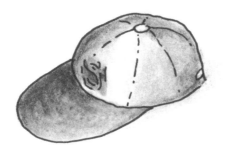

Oxford University Press

OXFORD

UNIVERSITY PRESS

Great Clarendon Street, Oxford OX2 6DP

Oxford University Press is a department of the Unversity of Oxford.
It furthers the University's objective of excellence in research, scholarship,
and education by publishing worldwide in

Oxford New York

Auckland Bangkok Buenos Aires Cape Town Chennai
Dar es Salaam Delhi Hong Kong Istanbul Karachi Kolkata
Kuala Lumpur Madrid Melbourne Mexico City Mumbai Nairobi
São Paulo Shanghai Taipei Tokyo Toronto

Oxford is a registered trade mark of Oxford University Press
in the UK and in certain other countries

ISBN 0 19 916873 3

Printed in Great Britain

Illustrations by Dee Shulman
Photograph of Michaela Morgan © Richard Drewe

Chapter 1

Look at the other kids in my class.

They have the right haircuts.
They have the right clothes – the jeans,
the t-shirts, the caps and the trainers.

These are my friends.

They may think I'm not all that big.

They may think I'm not all that
bright. But I know I'm really cool.
The trouble is my clothes are just
not cool at all.

'So what. I don't care,' I say to myself –
but I do care.

'You can wear my cap for today,' says
my best friend – but it's not the same.

My mum says,

My friend agrees with her. And I know
she's right too. It doesn't matter. It
shouldn't matter – but it does matter to
me.

I want to be like my friends.

I want to be cool.

In my mind I can see exactly what
I could look like.
And I say,

So I say, 'Can I have some t-shirts
like those?'

But she says, 'You've got plenty of your
cousins' old shirts that you haven't
grown into yet.'

And when I say, 'Look at those trainers, Mum. I don't suppose ...'

She says, 'I'm sorry, love. We just can't afford them.'

It seems that almost everything I have belonged to someone else before me.

And the fashions have changed a bit since my cousins were kids.

At school we all had to make up a rap about ourselves. This is mine:

Don't have the right sort of trainers
Don't have the right sort of hair
Don't have the right sort of labels
Pretend that I don't care.

BUT
Oh WOW!
Look at them now!
All the style
All the know-how –
Puma, Hi-tech and Reebok,
Cool as cool
They've got the
lot!

My friend says

But it's not such a good feeling.

Chapter 2

I know exactly what I want. I've seen them in a shop window.

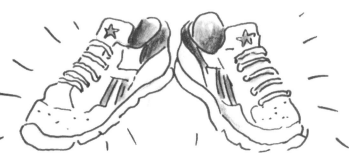

And I know exactly what my mum will say:

Money doesn't grow on trees you know.

We don't have money to burn!

Maybe for Christmas...

I dream about those trainers.

Maybe I could find some long lost treasure and buy them.

Maybe I could earn a reward and buy them.

Maybe I could get a job and ...

That's what I'll do!
I'll earn lots of money and buy my trainers.

It's not easy finding a job, especially when you're my age.

First I looked at the newspaper.

EXPERT SER

SITUATIONS VACANT

HYPNOTIST
Give up food
& smoking
Madame Gobb
Phone 31400

PLUMBER
Fix it Fa
call Paul

WANTED
Hairdresser's
Assistant
Suit
School-Leaver
Phone: FAY 16841

SECRETARY
Mature
lady
preferred
Tel. 42136

GARDENER NEEDED
Suit Old-Age Pensioner
APPLY PO BOX 143

WANTED
Shop Assistant
Saturday work
only
AGE 16+
Tel. 41360

SALESMAN/WOMAN
Experienced
sales staff
required
PHONE 813

BUS DRIVERS
If you have good driv
ills apply to join our
m. PHONE REG. 41311

They were all jobs for grown-ups or older kids. No good for me. What could I do?

I could look at the cards in the window of the corner shop.

There were plenty of cards:

For Sale
Table Tennis Table
by family moving
house with slightly
wobbly legs.
Tel. 33451

3 Adorable
baby rabbits
for sale.
Only £5 each.
Phone 42213
after 6

Typewriter for sale
Perfect working order
No good offers refused.

Phone 23%79$!

NEWSPAPER DELIVERY
BOYS AND GIRLS WANTED.

APPLY WITHIN

That's the one for me!

14

I'll get a job, save the money, and
I'll be Cool Clive
The Coolest Kid Alive.

But when I asked, the man said,

Outside the shop I met Rick Hamley from Mr Jacob's class. He had a newspaper round. He was dragging the bag behind him, and he was looking hot and tired.

6.30?

6.30!

Surely he didn't mean 6.30 in the morning!!!!

He did!

That night I was so excited I could hardly sleep. I'd asked my mum if I could help Rick with his paper round and, after a bit, she had agreed.

She helped me set the alarm clock for half past five and she made me go to bed extra early.

It's hard to go to sleep when it's still light. All my plans were racing through my head. They made a sort of song which went round and round and round …

I'll deliver the news
I'll earn money
I'll buy shoes
I'll buy trainers cool and snazzy
Big and bold and bright and jazzy
Imagine me when I get to school
Looking so great
Looking so cool.
Listen to the others
Hear them say
Look at Clive
Look at Clive
He's the coolest kid alive!

In the end I fell asleep, and then

It was time to get up and get started on my first week delivering the papers with Rick.

MONDAY
was very wet.

TUESDAY
was no better.

WEDNESDAY
was worse.

THURSDAY
was even wetter.

But I carried on …

FRIDAY ...	SATURDAY ....

On SUNDAY the newspapers are
very thick and heavy.

| I heaved that bag. | I hauled that bag. |

I nearly gave up, but I carried on and
I got paid. YIPPEE!

But the next day I met Rick...

23

Chapter 3

I went home and counted my money.

I made a special savings book and then I had a rest.

I was worn out and fed up and I still needed loads more money.

The next day I went back to the shop. I didn't go in, in case there were any more unhappy customers waiting for me, but I read the cards outside.

There were a few new ones.

For Sale
Set of Dining
Chairs by
family moving
house with
solid wooden
bottoms.
Tel. 33451

Baby rabbits
£3 each,
for quick sale.
Phone 42213
after 6

DOGWALKER WANTED
Give my dog one good
walk a day, and earn
extra pocket money.
34 PARK WALK, BARKWOOD

YES! That's the job for me!
I wrote down the address,
asked my mum, and went around
to see the lady.

'You're not very old,' she said. 'You're not very big … but you are the only one who's asked for the job … so I'll give you a try.'

Here's his lead and here's …

…Toodles!

'Now just take Toodles once around the park, then bring him straight back home. Don't get him tired. Don't get him dirty. Remember: once round the park and then straight back home … '

She told me what to do over and over
and over again. I wish she'd told the dog.
Toodles had a mind of his own.
We went once round the park.
No problem.

But then
Toodles decided to go round again

NO TOODLES!

and again ...

and again.

We visited the ducks. Toodles liked
the water.

We visited the gardens. Toodles liked
the mud and the manure.

We visited the litter bins. Toodles liked the rubbish.

Then Toodles decided to go home – the short way.

The lady was not pleased. Not pleased at all.

She gave me the money for one day but,

I went home, counted my money, filled in my book, then had a bath and a rest.

From time to time I went back to the shop. Sometimes there were new notices:

For Sale
Baby's cot by family moving house with a screw loose.
Tel. 33451

25 Rabbits FREE to a good home. Phone or call ANYTIME AT ALL 42213
47 Hutch Walk.

DUCKLINGS AND CHICKS GOING CHEAP.
TEL 89136

But there was only one job:

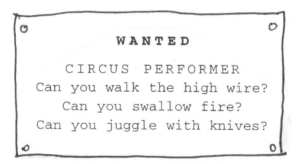

WANTED

CIRCUS PERFORMER
Can you walk the high wire?
Can you swallow fire?
Can you juggle with knives?

and that was NOT the job for me.

So I decided to start my own business.

I made posters:

and leaflets:

Your car was flashy
but now it's splashy
what do you do?

CALL FOR CLIVE

CLIVE'S CAR
CLEANING
AND ODD JOBS

phone 6 4 12 0

I borrowed some equipment –

a bucket,

a sponge

and a cloth

– and off I went.

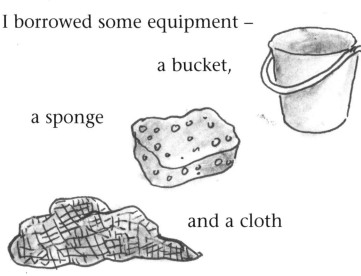

I was doing very well, very well indeed, when…

…I had …

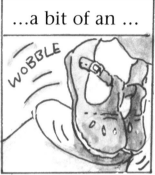

…a bit of an …

I was quite lucky really.
I didn't damage the car.
I didn't fall in the pond, but …

I did break a few things.

I said 'I'm very sorry …
It was an accident …
I'll pay for the damage.'

And I did.

Now all I had left was my soggy
sponge, my cloth, and my bucket with
a hole in it.

Can you imagine how I felt?

I was trudging home by the park when I heard:

Toodles! Come back!

Then:

OW! KEEP THAT DOG UNDER CONTROL!

And then:

SPLOSH!

A crowd of people were gathered by the duck pond. I went to have a look and got there just in time to see a man crawling out of the water. He was wet and covered in weeds. He didn't look happy at all.

Gaz and Rick were trying to pull
Toodles away and apologize to the
man at the same time.

Chapter 4

There in the middle of the pond was
his bag. It was bobbing about slowly
and drifting around in circles.

'It's full of very important papers,'
said the man. 'Oh no! It's going to sink!
Get a fishing net quick!' he yelled.

But no. The bag was sinking and no one had a fishing net.

But I did have an idea.

I used my cloth, my bucket with a hole in, and a long stick, and …

'Thank you. Thank you. THANK YOU!'
said the man. 'You've saved my bag and
all my papers and money. I would like to
reward you.'

He put his hand into his soggy bag and...

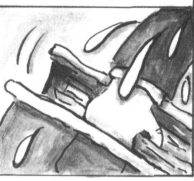

... I held my breath and wished.

Money? Money to buy my trainers?

Then he pulled out ...

a little soggy card

with an address on it.

'Pop in and see me,' he said.

And then he went leaving nothing behind but a patch of damp grass and some duckweed.

I went home and told my mum all about it.

So I had to wait till Saturday when she had the day off work.

In a way I was glad she'd come. It was a funny sort of place. It was a big warehouse in a side street, huge and dusty and full of boxes.

A bit spooky.

The man was busy telling me all about his job. 'I bring in all these things – some from other countries – and I sell them to shops.'

'I've seen some in shop windows,' I said.

'Help yourself to a few things then,' said the man.

'Oh we couldn't …' said my mum.

'Yes, you could,' agreed the man. 'Your boy saved me a lot of money and a lot of trouble. I want to reward him!'

So I got a cap and some jeans, a t-shirt and the trainers.

Cool!

In my new shirt I felt brighter.
In my new shoes I felt taller.
I looked the way I'd always felt I was –

Cool Clive,
the coolest kid alive!

About the author

I write all sorts of stories and I also like to write poems, so I particularly enjoyed writing Cool Clive, a story which has rhymes and raps in it.

I often visit schools and I got the idea for this story when I was talking to a group of children. I noticed that they were all wearing famous named trainers – all except one. I decided to write that boy's story.

Other books at Stages 12, 13, and 14 include:

Billy's Luck by Paul Shipton
Call 999! by Sylvia Moody
Front Page Story by Roger Stevens
Pet Squad by Paul Shipton
Sing for your Supper by Nick Warburton

Also available in packs
Stages 12/13/14 pack A   0 19 916879 2
Stages 12/13/14 class pack A   0 19 916880 6